Stop Defending - An Emotional
Self-Defense Guide

Stop Defending - An Emotional Self-Defense Guide

M J Meredith

CONTENTS

INTRODUCTION: YOU DON'T OWE ANYONE A DEFENSE

The Exhaustion of Justifying Yourself

Have you ever walked away from a conversation feeling drained, frustrated, or even ashamed, wondering why you spent so much time defending yourself?

Maybe a coworker made a snide remark about your work ethic, and instead of calling out their rudeness, you started explaining how busy you've been.

Maybe a family member criticised your life choices, and rather than holding your ground, you scrambled to justify yourself, hoping they'd stop judging you.

This is the exhausting cycle of *defending yourself*. And it's a trap.

Here's the truth:

You don't owe anyone an explanation for who you are.

You don't need to justify your choices, your feelings, or your existence.

Yet many of us have been conditioned to believe that when someone questions or criticises us, especially in a passive-aggressive or demeaning way. We must explain, defend, and prove ourselves.

But here's the problem:

Defending yourself doesn't work.

It:

- Puts you in a position of weakness
- Gives the other person control of the conversation
- Reinforces the idea that *their opinion of you* is something you need to address or correct

Author Note: I have a few sayings that help release me from the opinions of others. This is my favourite

"What you think about me is NONE of my business"

But what if, instead of defending... you flipped the script?

Emma's Awakening — A Case Study

Emma was always the quiet one in her group of friends. At work, she worked hard and kept her head down. At family gatherings, she was often teased.

> *"You're too sensitive, Emma."*
> *"Why are you always so quiet?"*
> *"You should speak up more!"*

Each time, she'd explain:

> *"I just don't like big crowds,"*
> *"I'm listening more than talking."*

But the teasing never stopped.

Then one day, Emma tried something different.

At a dinner party, a colleague laughed and said,

"Oh, Emma won't have an opinion, she never does."

Instead of defending herself, Emma calmly tilted her head and asked,

"Did you mean to say that out loud?"

There was an awkward silence. A few people laughed. The person who made the comment stammered,

"I was just joking."

Emma didn't smile. She simply asked,

"Oh? Why do you say that?"

The subject changed.
No more teasing that night.
For the first time, Emma didn't feel small. She felt powerful.

This book is about stepping into that same power.

Why We Defend Ourselves

To break the habit, we need to understand *why* we defend in the first place.

We've been trained to prioritise politeness and peacekeeping over personal boundaries.

We defend ourselves because:

- **We want approval.** We're raised to be likeable and deeply want to be seen in a positive light.

- **We've been conditioned to justify.** Children are constantly asked, *"Why did you do that?"* We grow up thinking we must always have an answer.
- **We feel guilty.** Maybe we think we *should* be doing more, working harder, making better choices. Maybe they're right? *(Hint: They're probably not.)*
- **We fear conflict.** Even though it's ineffective, defending can feel *safer* than confronting.
- **We don't know we have another option.** But we do. And this book will show you exactly how to use it.

Shifting the Power: Question Instead of Defend

Every time someone challenges you, you have three choices:

1. **Defend yourself.** (*Keeps you in a weak position.*)
2. **Stay silent.** (*Sometimes effective, but often unresolved.*)
3. **Flip the script and question them.**

This book is about **Option 3**.

When you question instead of defend, you *reclaim control* of the conversation.

Try This Instead

When someone says:

> *"You don't seem like you know what you're doing."*

Instead of defending, say:

> *"That's an interesting thing to say. Why do you think that?"*
> Or:
> *"Interesting view. Why do you say that?"*

Or if a relative says:

"You should be married by now."

Try:

"Oh? Why do you think that?"
(Then gently, again:)
"Yes, but why do you say that?"

Repeating the question shifts the focus onto them. It *makes them examine their own words*. It puts **you** in control.

Words That Weigh Us Down

We often carry words from others far longer than they do, words they likely don't even remember.

Their comment may have been careless or meaningless to them… but it can sting our soul and stay with us for years.

I call this:

Letting someone else rent space in your head.

Their words become internalised. They shape our confidence, our decisions, and how we see ourselves.

A Personal Story: Mr Nobody

When I was in high school, my English teacher (let's call him *Mr Nobody. Going Nowhere)* told me:

"You'll never write a complete sentence to save your life."

I was undiagnosed dyslexic at the time. His words weren't just unkind, they were devastating. That one remark shattered my confidence and silenced my creativity for *decades*.

I didn't write another story until I was in my 40s.

And yet... Here I am. Writing not just self-help books, but **novels**. Yes, plural.

Life Lesson: NEVER LET SOMEONE ELSES WORDS RENT SPACE IN YOUR HEAD.

Their opinion is not your truth. Your potential is not up for their judgement. The only person who gets to define what you're capable of is **you**.

What I Want To Share Within These Pages

This isn't a book about being rude, aggressive, or argumentative. It's about being clear, calm, and in control.

You'll learn how to:

- Stand your ground without guilt
- Respond with confidence, not explanations
- Challenge manipulative behaviour without losing your cool
- Protect your mental health and emotional energy

We'll tackle common scenarios, especially in **workplaces** and **families,** where emotional bullying thrives.

You'll also discover mindset tools like:

- **The Nike Moment** – Just do it. Stop overthinking
- **The Elsa Moment** – Let it go. Release resentment.

- *Worksheets and reflection exercises* to build your confidence step-by-step

Final Thought before we start

You don't need to defend your existence to *anyone*. You have just as much right to be here as anyone else.

And by the end of this book, you'll know **exactly** how to stand your ground. Without apology, without fear, and without a single defensive word.

Are you ready?

Let's begin.

Why We Defend Ourselves (And Why We Need to Stop)

The Invisible Trap of Defensiveness

Picture this:

You're at work, finishing a project you've put your heart into, when your manager walks by and says:

> *"This could have been done a little better, don't you think?"*

Your heart races. Before you can stop yourself, you say:

> *"Well, I had a lot of other tasks to juggle, and I followed the instructions exactly, and I was waiting on Sarah for her part, so I—"*

STOP.

Take a breath. Step back and ask yourself:

Why am I explaining myself?

Your manager didn't ask a question. They made a vague, slightly critical comment and somehow, you're suddenly justifying your existence.

This kind of interaction happens *all the time*. At work, at home, in friendships, even with strangers. Someone implies you're falling short, and your first instinct is to explain, defend, or justify.

Most of the time, they don't even realise, recognise or worst of all *remember* what they said.

But here's the truth:

You don't owe anyone a defence.

Defensiveness Feels Like Protection—But It's Not

We often don't realise when we're being defensive because it *feels* like we're standing up for ourselves.

But defensiveness isn't a strength. It's a reaction and it puts you in a position of weakness.

When you defend, you:

- Accept their framing of the conversation
- Grant their words more power than they deserve
- Hand them control of the narrative

Instead of defending, this book will help you flip the script. Calmly, clearly, and without apology.

Why Do We Defend Ourselves?

To stop a habit, we have to understand it. Most of our defensiveness comes from old wiring, deep-rooted beliefs shaped by our environment.

Here are the most common reasons:

1. We Want to Be Liked

Humans are wired for connection, we want to be accepted as part of the pack. Criticism, even subtle, feels like rejection. So we scramble to earn approval.

But here's the truth:

Not everyone will like you and that's *okay*.

(Apologies to the original authors. I can't recall where I first heard these, but they remind me of my value and sovereignty.)

2. We've Been Trained to Justify Ourselves

From a young age, we hear:

> *"Why did you do that?"*
> *"Explain yourself."*
> *"What's your excuse?"*

We grow up believing we must *always* have a reason. As adults, this turns into automatic over-explaining. Even when no explanation is required.

3. We Feel Guilty

Sometimes we *do* feel like we're falling short so when someone criticises us, we assume they're right.

But guilt isn't proof. It's just an emotion.

Don't let people weaponise your guilt to manipulate you.

4. We Fear Conflict

Many of us were raised to keep the peace at any cost. But constantly avoiding conflict teaches others they can walk all over us.

You don't need to start a fight but you do need to stop shrinking yourself to keep others comfortable.

5. We Haven't Learned Better Tools

Most of us think there are only two options:

- **Defend (and appear weak)**
- **Stay silent (and feel powerless)**

But there's a third, far more powerful option:

Flip the script. Question them instead.

A Better Strategy: Question Instead of Defend
Scenario:

You're at a family dinner. Your aunt leans in and says:

> *"You really should be married by now."*

Your instinct? Start explaining:

> *"Well, I've been focusing on my career, and dating is hard, and—"*

> **STOP.**

Try this instead:

> *"Oh? Why do you think that?"*

She might say:

"Well... it's just what people do."

You follow up with:

"Right, but why do you say that?"

This shifts the burden. You're not being rude. You're simply asking *them* to explain *their* outdated opinion.

Now *they* have to defend themselves.
You remain calm, confident, and in control.

Case Study: Mark's Workplace Victory

Mark was a reliable team player but his boss had a habit of making sly digs in meetings.

"Mark, I assume this report will actually be finished on time?"

Before, Mark would've scrambled:

"Well, last time was delayed because..."

But now, he paused and calmly asked:

"Are you saying you don't trust my ability to finish on time?"

The room fell silent.
His boss backtracked:

"No, no, I just meant I know things can get busy."

Mark nodded. The conversation moved on. No defending. No stress.

From that day forward, the digs stopped.

The Golden Rule of Emotional Self-Defence

When someone criticises, belittles, or embarrasses you, remember this:

The burden of explanation is on them. Not you.

Make *them* do the talking.

Try these:

- *"Oh? Why do you think that?"*

- *"Did you mean for that to sound so rude?"*

- *"That's an interesting assumption. Why do you say that?"*

- *"Did you mean to say that out loud?"* (*My personal favourite for confident moments!*)

These questions create a pause. Nine times out of ten, the other person will:

- **Get flustered**
- **Realise how rude they sounded**
- **Or drop the topic entirely**

And you? You stay powerful, calm, and clear.

Moving Forward

Now that you know why defensiveness is a trap, it's time to break free.

In Part 2, we'll dive into practical emotional self-defence strategies.

In Part 3, we'll explore how to handle common conflict zones: *work-places, families, and friendships.*

And in Part 4, we'll tackle the inner game: how to *stop procrastinating* and start owning your goals.

Keep in mind - You don't need to explain yourself to anyone.

You have just as much right to take up space as they do.

And by the end of this book, you'll know exactly how to do it. Without apology.

Mastering the Art of Emotional Self-Defense

You Don't Owe Anyone an Explanation

Let's start with a truth bomb:

You don't owe anyone an explanation for who you are, what you do, or the choices you make.

(Expect to hear this again, often.)

And yet, how often do we find ourselves justifying every detail of our lives?

- *"No, I'm not in a relationship right now, but I've been really focused on work."*
- *"I do still live in the same place, but housing prices are ridiculous."*
- *"Yes, I changed careers, but I wanted something more fulfilling."*

Why do we do this?

Because we've been conditioned to believe our choices are up for public debate. That when someone comments on our lives, we must *earn* their approval by explaining ourselves.

But here's the truth:

You don't.

If someone comments on your life, *it's not your job to justify yourself.* It's *their* job to explain why they think their opinion belongs in your space.

And *that*, right there, is the foundation of emotional self-defence.

The Three-Step Strategy for Emotional Self-Defence

You don't have to be aggressive to be assertive. You don't need to be loud to be powerful.

Here's a simple, repeatable three-step strategy to use every time you feel yourself slipping into defence mode.

Step 1: Recognise the Trap

Defensiveness is a knee-jerk reaction. The moment you catch yourself over-explaining, pause.

Ask yourself:

- *Am I answering a real question or defending myself?*

- *Do I actually owe this person an explanation?*

- *Would a confident version of me respond this way?*

If the answer is no. Stop mid-sentence if you have to and shift gears.

Step 2: Flip the Script

Put the pressure back on *them*. Do it calmly and confidently.

Here's how:

A. Ask a Question

- *"Why do you ask?"*

- *"What makes you say that?"*

- *"What do you mean by that?"*

   These prompt self-reflection and *return responsibility* to the speaker.

B. Call Out the Behaviour

- *"That's an interesting assumption. Why do you think that?"*

- *"Did you mean for that to sound rude?"*

- *"That's a bold statement. What's behind it?"*

   This style makes people think twice and they often backpedal.

C. Use Silence as a Weapon

Not every comment deserves a reply. Sometimes, no response is the most powerful one.

- *Pause. Raise an eyebrow. Wait.*

- *Use a slight head tilt (my personal go-to).*

- *If they push: "I don't think that deserves a response."*

Silence makes people uncomfortable. Especially those looking to provoke. Use it wisely.

Step 3: Walk Away Without Guilt

Once you've questioned or neutralised the comment, move on.

You do not need to:

- Keep explaining

- Fix their discomfort

- Soften the awkwardness

- Manage their feelings

Let them sit with the discomfort their own words created.
And don't let the moment rent space in your head, either. (This takes practice, but it leads you straight to confidence and clarity.)

Common Scenarios & How to Respond

Let's put emotional self-defence into practice.

Scenario 1: The Workplace Critic

Your boss or colleague says:

> *"You're always late with reports, aren't you?"*

Defensive Response:

"That's not true! I only missed one because—"

Emotionally Strong Response:

- *"Always? That's an interesting claim. When was the last time?"*

- *"Are you saying you're unhappy with my work? I'm happy to clarify expectations."*

Scenario 2: The Family Guilt Trip

Your parent says:

> *"You never come visit anymore."*

Defensive Response:

> *"I've just been so busy with work and—"*

Emotionally Strong Response:

- *"That's not true. When was the last time we caught up?"*

- *"I'd love to visit. Have you tried making plans with me?"*

Scenario 3: The Relationship Dig

A partner or friend says:

> *"You always overreact."*

Defensive Response:

> *"I don't! I just feel like you're not listening and—"*

Emotionally Strong Response:

- *"Interesting. What does 'overreacting' mean to you?"*

- *"Do you think dismissing my feelings helps us communicate better?"*

Case Study: Lisa & The Overbearing Relative

Lisa had an aunt who made every family gathering uncomfortable:

> *"Still single, Lisa? You'll run out of time soon!"*

Lisa used to laugh it off and say,

> *"I just haven't met the right person yet!"*

But then she learned emotional self-defence.

At the next gathering, her aunt made the same "joke."

Lisa smiled and asked:

> *"Oh? Why do you think that?"*

Her aunt blinked. "Well, it's just... people usually settle down by now."

Lisa tilted her head and said:

> *"But why does that matter to you?"*

Silence. The subject changed. And her aunt never brought it up again.

The Mindset Shift: From Defensive to Confident

At its heart, emotional self-defence isn't just about language. It's about mindset.

> **Stop assuming you need to justify yourself.**
> **Start assuming *others* should justify their opinions.**

When you embrace this shift:

- People stop trying to push your buttons

- You stay calm, clear, and in control

- You stop wasting energy on emotional drama

> **You have every right to live your life on your terms, no explanation required.**

Coming Up Next: Emotional Bullies & Power Games

Now that you know how to stop defending yourself, what about the people who push harder?

In Part 3, we'll dive deep into emotional bullies, toxic power dynamics, and how to neutralise their games. Whether they're in your family, your workplace, or your social circle.

By the time you're done with this book...
you'll be untouchable.

Emotional Bullies &
Power Games

What Is Emotional Bullying?

Emotional bullying isn't always loud or obvious. Sometimes, it's a **drip-feed of subtle digs, manipulative comments, or passive-aggressive behaviour** designed to make you doubt yourself.

Unlike physical bullying, emotional bullying leaves no bruises but plenty of scars.

It's:

- The offhand remark that lingers in your head for days

- The "joke" that isn't really a joke

- The guilt trip that makes you question whether you're a bad person

And the worst part? It often comes from the people closest to us family, partners, colleagues, even friends.
So how do you protect yourself without becoming cold, rude, or reactive?

Recognising the Power Games

Emotional bullies play games with one goal: **to control your emotions and dominate the conversation.** Once you see the game for what it is, you can break their power over you.

Here are the **most common tactics** and exactly how to shut them down.

1. The 'Just Joking' Jab

- "Wow, you actually look decent today."

- "No wonder you're still single!"

- "Relax, I was just joking. Don't be so sensitive."

A **disguised insult wrapped in humour.** And when you call it out, the bully flips it, accusing *you* of overreacting.

How to respond:

- "Oh, I love jokes! Tell me, where's the funny part?"

- "If you're joking, why am I not laughing?"

- *(Blank stare, then calmly change the subject.)*

   By not playing along, you strip away their power.

2. The Guilt Trip Gambit

- "After all I've done for you, this is how you treat me?"

- "Fine, do whatever you want. I guess I just don't matter."

- "If you really cared, you'd drop everything and help."

This tactic is **manipulation dressed as martyrdom.** The goal? Make *you* feel responsible for *their* emotions.

How to respond:

- "I can see you're upset, but my decision stands."

- "It sounds like you're trying to make me feel guilty. Is that your goal?"

- "I care about you, but I won't be guilted into something I don't want to do."

Guilt only works if you accept it. Don't.

3. The Backhanded Compliment

- "You're really brave to wear that."

- "You're actually pretty smart. For someone like you."

- "I didn't expect you to do so well. Good for you!"

These aren't compliments. They're **veiled put-downs**.

How to respond:

- "Oh, I didn't realise we were handing out insults today."

- "Thanks! That was *almost* a compliment."

- *(Big smile)* "Wow, that was a weird thing to say!"

Flip the awkwardness back on them.

4. The Gaslighting Game

- "That never happened. You're imagining things."

- "You're overreacting."

- "You always make a big deal out of nothing."

Gaslighting is designed to **make you question your reality.** The more confused you are, the easier you are to control.

How to respond:

- "That's not how I remember it."

- "It's interesting that you're dismissing my experience."

- "You don't have to agree, but don't tell me I'm wrong."

  Trust yourself. That's their greatest fear.

5. The Silent Treatment

- They stop talking to you after a disagreement

- They ignore your messages

- They act like you don't exist, until you apologise

This is emotional blackmail, **punishment through withdrawal.**

How to respond:

- "I can see you need space. I'll give it to you, but I won't beg for attention."

- "I don't respond to silent treatment. Let me know when you're ready to talk."

  They want you to chase. Don't.

Case Study: Tom & The Workplace Bully

Tom had a colleague "Greg" who was a **master of subtle digs**.
Every meeting, it was something like:

> "Oh, Tom actually had a good idea for once."

At first, Tom laughed along. But Greg didn't stop.

So one day, Tom calmly said:

> "Greg, I've noticed you do this a lot. Do you mean to sound condescending, or is that just your style?"

Silence.
Greg stammered, "I was just joking."
Tom shrugged. "Cool. Just checking."

Greg never pulled that stunt again.

Breaking the Cycle: How to Stay Unshakeable

Emotional bullies want one thing: **a reaction.** They want you to:

- Get flustered

- Defend yourself

- Feel small

Let's stop giving them what they want.

1. Don't Take the Bait

- Don't argue
- Don't explain
- Don't mirror their emotion

Stay calm, neutral, and unbothered.

2. Keep Your Boundaries Firm

- If someone keeps making comments about your weight, job, or love life, tell them *once* that it's off-limits.

- If they do it again, say:

> "We're done with this conversation."
> **And walk away.**

3. Detach from Their Approval

Bullies rely on your **need for validation**.
The moment you stop needing their approval, they lose control.

- "I don't need their approval. Their opinion is **irrelevant**."

(Write that down. Repeat it often.)

And let's be real, what's to admire in someone who makes a sport of tearing others down?

Moving Forward: Emotional Strength as a Lifestyle

Emotional self-defence isn't just about confrontation.
It's about living in a way that says:

- "I know who I am."

- "I don't explain myself to people who try to tear me down."

- "I don't carry other people's projections."

When you integrate these techniques into your life:

- Bullies stop targeting you

- Conversations become more honest

- You stop wasting energy on emotional drama

You don't just feel stronger. You *are* stronger.

Coming Up Next: Procrastination & Personal Growth

Now that you know how to disarm emotional bullies, it's time to focus inward.

In **Part 4**, we'll tackle procrastination:

- Why we do it

- How to beat it

- And how to finally move toward the life you want

No more stalling. No more shrinking. It's time to act.

Procrastination &
Personal Growth

Why Talk About Procrastination?

> "They said you'd never finish. Prove them wrong by starting anyway."

You might wonder why I've included a chapter on procrastination in a book about emotional self-defence. But here's the truth: when you've spent years (or even decades) giving away your power, it changes you. You start to shrink yourself. You begin to second-guess your instincts. Sometimes you even forget what it felt like to chase something just for the joy of it.

That loss often begins with the slow drip of snide remarks or veiled digs from others. Comments that imply we're not enough, not capable, or simply not cut out for something bigger. And over time, we start treating those comments as fact. We internalise their criticism and add our own dreams to the ever-growing pile of things we were "never going to finish anyway."

This is where procrastination takes hold. Not just as a bad habit, but as a form of quiet self-sabotage that protects us from the sting of failure or worse, the judgement we imagine will follow success. It can feel safe, even justified. But make no mistake, it's also reinforcing every limiting belief someone else planted in our path.

So before we move forward with tools to reclaim your time and energy, let's pause here. Let's take a closer look at procrastination. Not just what it is, but why it shows up, and how we can stop letting it speak louder than our potential.

Why Do We Procrastinate?

Let's get one thing straight: procrastination isn't laziness.
It's often a signal of fear, perfectionism, burnout, or misalignment.

We procrastinate because:

- It feels overwhelming – You don't know where to start, so you don't start at all.

- You're afraid of failure – If you never try, you can't fail... right?

- You're afraid of success – What if you succeed and now people expect more? (Hello, imposter syndrome.)

- You're waiting for the 'right time' – Spoiler: it never comes.

- You don't actually want to do it – You're forcing yourself to care about something that doesn't align with your values.

Here's the truth:

66 **Procrastination is a thief.** 99

It steals your time, your energy, and your potential.

The 'Nike Moment': Just Do It

Not every task needs deep emotional analysis.
Some things just need doing.

Enter your Nike Moment, the instant you stop overthinking and start acting.

The 5-Minute Rule

- If a task feels overwhelming, tell yourself you'll just do it for five minutes.

- No pressure to finish. Just begin.

- Most of the time? You'll keep going.

Examples:

- Dreading that email? Just open the draft and write one line.

- Avoiding exercise? Just put on your shoes and stretch.

- Stressed about a phone call? Just dial the number.

The first step kills procrastination.

The 'Elsa Moment': Let It Go

Sometimes, procrastination is less about laziness and more about fear of judgement, rejection, or failure. That's where what I call the *Elsa moment* comes in.

In Disney's *Frozen*, Elsa reaches a turning point when she stops hiding her power and belts out the iconic anthem *Let It Go*. It's more than a catchy tune, it's a declaration of release. She sheds the expectations, shame, and fear that kept her small, and finally steps into her truth.

That's what the *Elsa moment* is all about: choosing to let go of other people's opinions, past criticism, and self-doubt so you can own your voice and move forward. This isn't just about singing in the snow, this is about your life. What are you ready to let go of today?

No remember not every task or thought from the past is worthy of your energy.
Sometimes, procrastination is your intuition tapping you on the shoulder, saying: *"This isn't for you."*

Ask yourself:

- *Do I actually need to do this?*

- *Is this my goal—or someone else's expectation?*

- *What happens if I just... let it go?*

You don't have to fight every battle.
Choose wisely. Reclaim your energy.

How to Build Momentum

Once you've kicked procrastination to the curb, you need a way to stay in motion.

Here's how:

1. **Set 'Embarrassingly Small' Goals**

   Bad goal: "I'll write a book this year."
   Good goal: "I'll write 200 words today."

   Bad goal: "I want to get fit."
   Good goal: "I'll do 10 squats before breakfast."

Make it too small to fail. Tiny wins build momentum and confidence.

2. Use the 'Future You' Trick

Imagine Future You—just one week from now.
Would they be:

(Positive) *Relieved* that you got it done today?

(Negative) Or *annoyed* that you didn't?

Ask:

◇ "Am I screwing over Future Me?"

If the answer is yes—just do it now.

3. Don't Wait for Motivation

Motivation is flaky. It's not a strategy, it's a mood.

Instead, build systems:

- Put your gym clothes next to your bed—no decision needed.

- Use alarms or reminders—don't rely on memory.

- Work in a focused space—don't debate with distraction.

Action creates momentum. Systems keep it going.

Case Study: Sophie & the Overwhelming To-Do List

Sophie always dreamed of starting her own jewellery business.
But her brain was full of noise:

- "I don't know where to start."

- "I'm not good enough."

- "Maybe next year."

One day, Sophie gave herself a Nike Moment.
She told herself:

"I'll just sketch one design today. That's it."

The next day? Another sketch.
Then she researched materials. Then she bought supplies.
Within six months, she launched her first collection.

The turning point?
She stopped overthinking. She started acting.

Turning Procrastination Into Progress

If you take one thing from this chapter, let it be this:

- Stop waiting for the perfect time. The right time is *now*.

- Start small. Tiny steps build massive momentum.

- Let go of what doesn't matter. Focus your energy where it *does*.

When you take control of your time, you take control of your life.

Your Turn: Reflection Prompt

What's one small action you've been putting off? One task that would make Future You breathe easier?

Write it down.

Now commit to just five minutes.
No pressure to finish. Just start.
You don't need permission to move forward—just momentum.

*Coming Up Next: Standing Your Ground & Living
Confidently*

Now that you've kicked procrastination to the curb, it's time to step up
and own your space.

In Part 5, we'll dive into:

- How to set boundaries (without guilt)

- How to own your space in any room

- How to stop apologising for being yourself

No more playing small.
It's time to live confidently and unapologetically.

Apology to Authority - Standing Your Ground

The Power of Owning Your Space

There's a big difference between being aggressive and standing your ground.

- **Aggressive people** push others down to feel powerful.

- **Confident people** stand tall and refuse to be pushed.

This chapter is about **owning your space**, setting boundaries, and walking through life **unapologetically**.

Because you don't owe anyone an explanation for who you are.

Step 1: Stop Over-Apologising

Ever caught yourself saying "sorry" when you weren't actually sorry?

- "Sorry, can I just squeeze past?" (Why apologise for existing?)

- "Sorry, I just think..." (Why soften your opinion?)

- "Sorry I didn't see your message!" (Why apologise for not being constantly available?)

Let's flip that:

Instead of "Sorry, can I just squeeze past?"
Try "Excuse me."

Instead of "Sorry, I just think..."
Try "Here's my opinion."

Instead of "Sorry I didn't see your message!"
Try "Just saw this now. What's up?"

Apologise **only** when it's necessary.
Don't apologise for **taking up space**.

Step 2: Set Boundaries Without Guilt

A boundary is **a line you protect**. It tells others: *"This is where I end and you begin."*

- If someone talks over you. **Call it out.**

- If someone makes a rude comment. **Don't laugh it off**

- If someone pushes your limits. **Stand firm.**

How to Set a Boundary in One Sentence

- "I don't like when you [behaviour]. Please stop."

- "That's not okay with me."

- "I won't discuss this further."

No explanations. No apologies. Just clarity.

Step 3: Call Out Rude Behaviour (Without Defending Yourself)

Some people get away with bad behaviour because no one challenges them.

Instead of **defending**, try **questioning**.

defending "That's not true! I didn't do that!"
questioning "Why do you feel the need to say that?"

defending "I don't think that's fair!"
questioning "What do you mean by that?"

This flips the spotlight onto *their* behaviour. Not yours.

Step 4: Own Your Space in Conversations

Confident people:

- **DO NOT** Speak fast to avoid interruption

- **DO NOT** Shrink in the room

- **DO NOT** Let others dominate the conversation

Instead:

- **Speak slower** – rushing signals doubt

- **Pause after making a point** – let your words land

- **Hold eye contact** – it shows presence and self-trust

Confidence isn't just **what** you say.
It's **how** you say it.

Case Study: Liam & The Workplace Bully

Liam had a co-worker who constantly undermined him:

- Took credit for his ideas

- Talked over him in meetings

- Made passive-aggressive jabs

Liam used to stay quiet, hoping to keep the peace.
Until one day:

Co-worker: "Oh, I thought you'd already stuffed that up."
Liam: "Did you mean to say that out loud?"

Silence.
Then nervous laughter.

From that day on, the bullying stopped.
Sometimes, **one calm question** changes everything.

The Final Step: Walk Through Life Unapologetically

If you take **one thing** from this book, let it be this:

- You don't need to **justify who you are**

- You don't have to **shrink to keep others comfortable**

- You have **every right** to take up space

Confidence isn't being the loudest person in the room.
It's quietly knowing your worth and acting like it.

Your Turn: Confidence Workbook

Let's put this into practice:

Step 1: Identify the Pattern

What's one situation where you often feel the need to apologise, justify, or shrink yourself?

Example:

"I always let my friend talk over me because I don't want to seem rude."

Step 2: Choose Your New Response

Write a confident response you'll try next time.

Example:

"I'm still speaking. Let me finish."

Small shifts create big change.
Before long, you'll be walking taller. Inside and out.

Coming Up Next: The Wrap-Up & Moving Forward

Now that you know how to stand your ground, it's time to bring it all together.

In the final chapter, we'll explore:
◇ How to keep your confidence growing
◇ How to handle setbacks and self-doubt
◇ How to apply emotional self-defence in **every area** of life

Because this isn't just a book, it's a toolkit.
And now, you know how to use it.

This is just the Beginning

You've made it through this book.

That means you're ready to **stop defending yourself** and start **owning your space**.

Because here's the truth:

- You don't have to justify who you are.
- You don't owe anyone an explanation for existing.
- You have the right to set boundaries, say no, and expect respect.

This isn't about being aggressive. It's about **knowing your worth and acting like it.**

1. Confidence Is a Skill—Keep Practicing

Confidence isn't something you're born with. It's a **muscle** you build.

At first, it might feel weird to:

- Say, "I don't accept that," instead of explaining yourself.

- Ask, "Why do you say that?" instead of getting defensive.

- Stand firm instead of apologising for everything.

But every time you practise these techniques, you get stronger.

Confidence is like learning to swim.
You don't wait until you're fearless to jump in.
You **jump in** and become fearless *by swimming*.

2. Setbacks Will Happen—That's Normal

Not every comeback will land.
Not every boundary will be respected.
Not every conversation will go your way.

And that's okay.

Confidence isn't about being perfect.
It's about **trusting you can handle what comes next**.

So if something doesn't go to plan?

- Learn from it.

- Adjust.

- Try again.

3. Your Voice Matters—Use It

Some people won't like the new, confident you.

- They're used to you being quiet.

- They're used to you apologising.

- They're used to you shrinking yourself.

That's **their** problem. Not yours.

You have just as much right to take up space as anyone else.

4. *Your Life, Your Rules*

This book gave you tools to:

- **Stop apologising for existing**

- **Set boundaries without guilt**

- **Flip the script on emotional bullies**

- **Navigate workplace and family conflict**

- **Move towards your goals without fear**

Now it's your turn to **use them**.

No more defending.
No more explaining.

Just **standing tall** and **owning your life**.

Final Exercise: Your Power Statement

Write your own **power statement**. A declaration of the new, confident you.

Example:

"I am strong. I don't need to explain myself. I set boundaries and expect respect. I am in control of my life."

Say it out loud.
Say it often.
Say it until you **believe it**.

Because once you do, **everything changes**.

One Last Thing...

This isn't the end.
It's the beginning.

Go out there.
Live unapologetically.
And most importantly—

Stop defending. Start owning your space.

" Personal Note from the Author   "

This book is about emotional bullying and reclaiming your emotional well-being.

But if you are in a **physically or financially abusive** situation, your safety comes first.

I know it can feel overwhelming or even impossible right now but please know: **you deserve better.**

It may take time, and the journey may be hard. But with **support, courage, and the right** help, you *will* find your way to a better place.

You are strong.
You are worthy.
You deserve to feel safe and respected.

Don't be afraid to reach out, to a trusted friend, a counsellor, or a support organisation. You are not alone.
And you are never beyond help.

Your story isn't over.

"Emotional Intelligence: Why It Can Matter More Than IQ" by Daniel Goleman

"The Gifts of Imperfection" by Brené Brown

"The Assertiveness Workbook: How to Express Your Ideas and Stand Up for Yourself at Work and in Relationships" by Randy J. Paterson

"The Dance of Anger: A Woman's Guide to Changing the Patterns of Intimate Relationships" by Harriet Lerner

"The Art of Saying No: How to Set Healthy Boundaries and Stop People-Pleasing" by Damon Zahariades

"Nonviolent Communication: A Language of Life" by Marshall B. Rosenberg

"Emotional Bullies: Dealing with the People Who Hurt You" by Jodie Gale

"Toxic Workplace! Managing Toxic Personalities and Their Systems of Power" by Mitchell Kusy & Elizabeth Holloway

"Dare to Lead: Brave Work. Tough Conversations. Whole Hearts." by Brené Brown

"The Bully, the Bullied, and the Bystander" by Barbara Coloroso

"The No Asshole Rule: Building a Civilized Workplace and Surviving One That Isn't" by Robert I. Sutton

"Atomic Habits: An Easy & Proven Way to Build Good Habits & Break Bad Ones" by James Clear

"The War of Art: Break Through the Blocks and Win Your Inner Creative Battles" by Steven Pressfield

"The 5 Second Rule: Transform Your Life, Work, and Confidence with Everyday Courage" by Mel Robbins

"Getting Things Done: The Art of Stress-Free Productivity" by David

Allen

"The Self-Esteem Workbook" by Glenn R. Schiraldi

"Radical Acceptance: Embracing Your Life With the Heart of a Buddha" by Tara Brach

"You Are a Badass: How to Stop Doubting Your Greatness and Start Living an Awesome Life" by Jen Sincero

Psychology Today - Articles on Emotional Intelligence & Assertiveness by Various Authors

Mind Tools - Assertiveness Techniques & Building Confidence by Various Authors

www.ingramcontent.com/pod-product-compliance
Lightning Source LLC
Chambersburg PA
CBHW031135020426
42333CB00012B/391